W9-ANU-241

WEEKLY WR READER®
EARLY LEARNING LIBRARY

My Day at School/

Mi día en la escuela

Eating Lunch at School/
El almuerzo en la escuela

by/por Joanne Mattern

Reading consultant/Consultora de lectura:
Susan Nations, M.Ed.,
author, literacy coach,
consultant in literacy development/
autora, tutora de alfabetización,
consultora de desarrollo de la lectura

Please visit our web site at: www.garethstevens.com
For a free color catalog describing Weekly Reader® Early Learning Library's list
of high-quality books, call 1-877-445-5824 (USA) or 1-800-387-3178 (Canada).
Weekly Reader® Early Learning Library's fax: (414) 336-0164.

Library of Congress Cataloging-in-Publication Data

Mattern, Joanne, 1963
   [Eating lunch at school. Spanish & English]
   Eating lunch at school = El almuerzo en la escuela / by/por Joanne Mattern.
     p. cm. – (My day at school = Mi día en la escuela)
   Includes bibliographical references and index.
   ISBN-10: 0-8368-7358-0 — ISBN-13: 978-0-8368-7358-0 (lib. bdg.)
   ISBN-10: 0-8368-7365-3 — ISBN-13: 978-0-8368-7365-8 (softcover)
   1. School children—Food—Juvenile literature. 2. School children—Juvenile literature. I. Title.
II. Title: Almuerzo en la escuela. III. Series: Mattern, Joanne, 1963- My day at school.
LB3475.M2818   2007
371.7'16—dc22   2006017290

This edition first published in 2007 by
Weekly Reader® Early Learning Library
A Member of the WRC Media Family of Companies
330 West Olive Street, Suite 100
Milwaukee, WI 53212 USA

Copyright © 2007 by Weekly Reader® Early Learning Library

Editor: Barbara Kiely Miller
Art direction: Tammy West
Cover design and page layout: Kami Strunsee
Picture research: Diane Laska-Swanke
Photographer: Gregg Andersen
Translators: Tatiana Acosta and Guillermo Gutiérrez

Printed in the United States of America

1 2 3 4 5 6 7 8 9 10 09 08 07 06

Note to Educators and Parents

Reading is such an exciting adventure for young children! They are beginning to integrate their oral language skills with written language. To encourage children along the path to early literacy, books must be colorful, engaging, and interesting; they should invite the young reader to explore both the print and the pictures.

The *My Day at School* series is designed to help young readers review the routines and rules of a school day, while learning new vocabulary and strengthening their reading comprehension. In simple, easy-to-read language, each book follows a child through part of a typical school day.

Each book is specially designed to support the young reader in the reading process. The familiar topics are appealing to young children and invite them to read — and re-read — again and again. The full-color photographs and enhanced text further support the student during the reading process.

In addition to serving as wonderful picture books in schools, libraries, homes, and other places where children learn to love reading, these books are specifically intended to be read within an instructional guided reading group. This small group setting allows beginning readers to work with a fluent adult model as they make meaning from the text. After children develop fluency with the text and content, the book can be read independently. Children and adults alike will find these books supportive, engaging, and fun!

— Susan Nations, M.Ed., author, literacy coach,
and consultant in literacy development

Nota para los maestros y los padres

¡Leer es una aventura tan emocionante para los niños pequeños! A esta edad están comenzando a integrar su manejo del lenguaje oral con el lenguaje escrito. Para animar a los niños en el camino de la lectura incipiente, los libros deben ser coloridos, estimulantes e interesantes; deben invitar a los jóvenes lectores a explorar la letra impresa y las ilustraciones.

La serie *Mi día en la escuela* está pensada para ayudar a los jóvenes lectores a repasar las actividades y normas de un día de escuela, mientras enriquecen su vocabulario y refuerzan su comprensión. Cada libro presenta, en un lenguaje sencillo y fácil de entender, las actividades de un niño durante parte de un típico día escolar.

Cada libro está especialmente diseñado para ayudar al joven lector en el proceso de lectura. Los temas familiares llaman la atención de los niños y los invitan a leer —y releer— una y otra vez. Las fotografías a todo color y el tamaño de la letra ayudan aún más al estudiante en el proceso de lectura.

Además de servir como maravillosos libros ilustrados en escuelas, bibliotecas, hogares y otros lugares donde los niños aprenden a amar la lectura, estos libros han sido especialmente concebidos para ser leídos en un grupo de lectura guiada. Este contexto permite que los lectores incipientes trabajen con un adulto que domina la lectura mientras van determinando el significado del texto. Una vez que los niños dominan el texto y el contenido, el libro puede ser leído de manera independiente. ¡Estos libros les resultarán útiles, estimulantes y divertidos a niños y a adultos por igual!

— Susan Nations, M.Ed., autora/tutora de alfabetización/
consultora de desarrollo de la lectura

The school bell rings. It is time for **lunch**.

Suena la campana de la escuela. Es la hora del **almuerzo**.

I get in line with my class. We walk to the **cafeteria**, or lunchroom. We are quiet in the halls.

Me pongo en fila con mi clase. Caminamos hasta la **cafetería**, o comedor. En los pasillos estamos callados.

Some children buy lunch. Today's lunch is pizza.

Algunos niños compran el almuerzo.

El almuerzo de hoy es pizza.

We can buy milk and juice at school. I like chocolate milk the best.

En la escuela podemos comprar leche y jugos. La leche chocolatada es mi preferida.

I brought my lunch from home.

I have a **sandwich**. I have fruit.

Yo traje mi almuerzo de casa.

Tengo un **sándwich**. Tengo fruta.

Mom packed **pudding**, too!

I love pudding!

- - - - - - - - - - - - - - - - -

¡Mamá también metió **pudín**!

¡Me encanta el pudín!

I sit at a table with my friends.

We eat and talk.

— — — — — — — — — — — — — —

Me siento a una mesa con mis

amigos. Comemos y platicamos.

I clean up after I finish my lunch.

I throw away my **trash**.

Después del almuerzo, recojo.

Tiro la **basura**.

Lunch is over. We line up to go outside. Now we can play!

El almuerzo terminó. Nos ponemos en fila para salir fuera. ¡Ahora podemos jugar!

Glossary

buy — to get something by paying money for it

cafeteria — a place where people buy food that is ready to eat

class — a group of students who are learning together

lunch — a meal eaten in the middle of the day

pudding — a sweet, creamy dessert

sandwich — two slices of bread with meat or another filling in between

trash — things to be thrown away

Glosario

almuerzo — comida que se hace a mediodía

basura — cosas que hay que tirar

cafetería — lugar donde se puede comprar comida lista para comer

clase — grupo de estudiantes que aprenden juntos

comprar — pagar dinero para obtener algo

pudín — postre dulce y cremoso

sándwich — dos rebanadas de pan con algo de carne o de otro relleno en el centro

For More Information/Más información

Books

Fruit. Let's Read About Food (series). Cynthia Klingel (Gareth Stevens)

Milk and Cheese. Let's Read About Food (series). Cynthia Klingel (Gareth Stevens)

School Lunch. True Kelley (Holiday House)

Libros

Comiendo bien. Lisa Trumbauer (Capstone Press)

Las frutas. Los grupos de alimentos (series). Robin Nelson (Lerner)

Index

Índice

About the Author

Joanne Mattern has written more than one hundred and fifty books for children. Joanne also works in her local library. She lives in New York State with her husband, three daughters, and assorted pets. She enjoys animals, music, going to baseball games, reading, and visiting schools to talk about her books.

Información sobre la autora

Joanne Mattern ha escrito más de ciento cincuenta libros para niños. Además, Joanne trabaja en la biblioteca de su comunidad. Vive en el estado de Nueva York con su esposo, sus tres hijas y varias mascotas. A Joanne le gustan los animales, la música, ir al béisbol, leer y hacer visitas a las escuelas para hablar de sus libros.